Florida

Jim Ollhoff

Visit us at
www.abdopublishing.com

Published by ABDO Publishing Company, 8000 West 78th Street, Suite 310, Edina, Minnesota 55439 USA. Copyright ©2010 by Abdo Consulting Group, Inc. International copyrights reserved in all countries. No part of this book may be reproduced in any form without written permission from the publisher. The Checkerboard Library™ is a trademark and logo of ABDO Publishing Company.

Printed in the United States.

Editor: John Hamilton
Graphic Design: Sue Hamilton
Cover Illustration: Neil Klinepier
Cover Photo: iStock Photo

Manufactured with paper containing at least 10% post-consumer waste

Interior Photo Credits: Alamy, AP Images, Comstock, Corbis, David Olson, Florida Marlins, Getty, Granger Collection, Gunter Küchler, iStock Photo, Jacksonville Jaguars, John Hamilton, Library of Congress, Megan Prusynski, Miami Dolphins, Miami Heat, Mile High Maps, NASA, Mountain High Maps, One Mile Up, Orlando Magic, Peter Arnold Inc., Tampa Bay Buccaneers, Tampa Bay Rays, Tom Joseph, and U.S. Postal Service.

Statistics: State population statistics taken from 2008 U.S. Census Bureau estimates. City and town population statistics taken from July 1, 2007, U.S. Census Bureau estimates. Land and water area statistics taken from 2000 Census, U.S. Census Bureau.

Library of Congress Cataloging-in-Publication Data

Ollhoff, Jim, 1959-
  Florida / Jim Ollhoff.
      p. cm. -- (The United States)
  Includes index.
  ISBN 978-1-60453-644-7
  1. Florida--Juvenile literature. I. Title.

F311.3.O44 2010
975.9--dc22
                            2008051031

Table of Contents

The Sunshine State

Florida is the southernmost of the 48 connected states. It is a major vacation spot because of the climate and the many amusement parks and activities.

Spanish explorer Juan Ponce de León sailed to Florida in 1513. He landed on Florida's east coast, near the present-day city of St. Augustine. Because he saw so many flowers, he named the new territory *La Florida,* which means "The Flower" in Spanish.

Florida is sometimes called the "Sunshine State," because of the climate. It is sunny and mild much of the year. Bad weather can happen, of course, but people like to think of Florida as sunny all the time.

A man relaxes at Florida's Bahia Honda State Park.

Quick Facts

Name: From the Spanish words *La Florida*, meaning "the flower," because the first explorers saw so many wild flowers.

State Capital: Tallahassee, population 168,979

Date of Statehood: March 3, 1845 (27th state)

Population: 18,328,340 (4th-most populous state)

Area (Total Land and Water): 65,755 square miles (170,305 sq km), 22nd-largest state

Largest City: Jacksonville, population 805,605

Nickname: The Sunshine State

Motto: In God We Trust

State Bird: Mockingbird

FLORIDA

State Flower: Orange Blossom

State Rock: Agatized Coral

State Tree: Sabal Palm

State Song: "Swanee River"

Highest Point: Britton Hill, 345 feet (105 m)

Lowest Point: At the Coast, 0 feet (0 m)

Agatized Coral

Average July Temperature: 75°F (24°C)

Record High Temperature: 109°F (43°C), at Monticello, June 29, 1931

Average January Temperature: 68°F (20°C)

Record Low Temperature: –2°F (19°C), at Tallahassee, February 13, 1899

Sabal Palm

Average Annual Precipitation: 53 inches (135 cm)

Number of U.S. Senators: 2

Number of U.S. Representatives: 25

U.S. Postal Service Abbreviation: FL

Geography

Florida has more than 8,400 miles (13,518 km) of shoreline.

Most of Florida is a large peninsula, jutting out into the ocean. It has more than 8,400 miles (13,518 km) of shoreline. Only Alaska has more shoreline than Florida. To the west of Florida is the Gulf of Mexico. To the east of Florida is the Atlantic Ocean. To the north are the states of Alabama and Georgia.

The northern part of Florida has more hills than the rest of the state. However, the highest point in Florida is near Alabama, and it is only 345 feet (105 m) above sea level. The land directly south of Alabama and western Georgia is called the panhandle.

Florida's total land and water area is 65,755 square miles (170,305 sq km). It is the 22nd-largest state. The state capital is Tallahassee.

The southern part of Florida is mostly flat. The southern-most part of Florida is called the Everglades. It is filled with swamps and marshland. Everglades National Park is at the southern part of this area.

At the very southern tip of Florida is a string of islands called the Florida Keys. They are popular tourist spots. A highway connects many of the islands.

A heron in Everglades National Park.

Florida has thousands of lakes, and almost 2,000 streams. The Saint John's River is the longest, measuring 300 miles (483 km). Lake Okeechobee is the largest lake. It is northwest of Miami, in the southern part of the state. The lake covers about 730 square miles (1,891 sq km), but only has an average depth of 9 feet (3 m). Florida also has many natural springs that bubble up from underground lakes.

A view of Florida from space.

Climate and Weather

In the winter, southern Florida is often the warmest place in the United States. January temperatures are usually about 70 degrees Fahrenheit (21°C) or higher. In northern Florida, January temperatures average around 54 degrees Fahrenheit (12°C). Sometimes the weather in northern Florida drops below freezing.

In summer, the temperatures are around 80 degrees Fahrenheit (27°C) in the south. The breezes coming from

Florida's ocean breezes keep the weather warm.

the ocean keep the temperature from getting too hot. It rarely drops below freezing in the southern part of the state. The Florida Keys have never had frost for as long as scientists have kept records.

Florida is often hit with dangerous hurricanes. These huge storms form in the Atlantic Ocean and move westward. Sometimes Florida is in their path. Hurricanes break up quickly over land, but they can do a lot of damage before they disappear.

A trampoline is blown away during Hurricane Wilma in Boca Raton, Florida, in 2005.

Plants and Animals

Florida has many different types of land, so it also has many different kinds of plants and animals.

Almost half of Florida is forest. Common trees in the state include longleaf pine, pond pine, oaks, cypresses, palms, and mangroves. Common trees in the south include the hickory, red maple, sweet gum, tulip, and magnolia. Nearly half of all tree species in the United States can be found in Florida.

The Everglades area is filled with animals because few humans live there. Crocodiles and alligators are found in the Everglades. Raccoons, skunks, bobcats, and deer live there also.

Florida is home to many thousands of birds. Pelicans, egrets, herons, ibises, spoonbills, and flamingoes are a few.

Florida's Everglades is the only place where <u>both</u> crocodiles and alligators live.

Dolphin

Magnolia

Flamingo

Manatee

Key deer

Florida's waterways hold many varieties of fish, as well as bottlenose dolphins and West Indian manatees. The manatee, sometimes called a sea cow, was once hunted nearly to extinction. Today, they are an endangered species. The small Key deer is found in the Florida Keys.

In the northern part of the state, black bears inhabit the forests. Gray foxes, otters, armadillos, boars, and bobcats can also be found.

There are 40 different kinds of snakes in Florida. Water moccasins, coral snakes, and rattlesnakes are poisonous.

A water moccasin.

The Florida panther, sometimes called the puma or cougar, is the official state animal. Florida is the only state east of the Mississippi River where this animal roams. It can grow up to six feet (2 m) long or more. Its main food is the white-tailed deer. It is an endangered species, which means conservation organizations are trying to protect the animals. Probably less than 100 live in the wild.

Florida panther

Loss of habitat, traffic accidents, and disease have made the Florida panther one of the most endangered mammals on Earth. It is estimated that less than 100 live in the wild.

History

People lived in Florida 12,000 years ago, and probably earlier. They were called Paleo-Indians. They were the ancestors of the Native Americans.

When the first Europeans came, there were about 350,000 Native Americans living in Florida. These people included the Timucua, Apalachee, and Calusa Indians. Later, Creek Indians from Georgia came to live in the area. The tribes began to live together and all became known as the Seminole Indians.

Seminoles fish during the 1500s.

Juan Ponce de León first explored Florida in 1513. He landed on the east coast, near today's city of St. Augustine. He returned in 1521 to explore the west side of Florida, near present-day Fort Myers. In 1528, another Spanish ship landed in the area of Tampa. In 1539, there was another attempted settlement, and another in 1549. The French attempted to settle near modern-day Jacksonville.

The Spanish explorer Juan Ponce de León was the first European to explore Florida. He landed on the east coast, near today's city of St. Augustine.

For years, the Seminoles defended their lands against European settlers.

European settlements weren't always successful. The Seminoles defended their lands. The settlers were often unprepared. Hurricanes sometimes wiped out settlements. For 250 years, the British, French, and Spanish fought each other for control of Florida.

By the mid-1700s, most of the Native Americans had died from wars and European diseases. In the early 1800s, the United States government forced most of the Seminoles to accept a treaty that made them move to a reservation in Oklahoma.

By 1821, the Spanish gave up their claims to Florida. The United States took possession of it. The United States government admitted Florida as the 27th state in 1845.

In the early 1800s, many of the Southern states wanted to keep slavery legal. Farmers in the South had very large farms called plantations. They claimed they needed slaves to work their plantations. In 1861, many Southern states left the Union, beginning the Civil War. Florida was one of the states that joined the Confederacy. Much of the Civil War was fought north of Florida. Some of the coastal cities of Florida were occupied by Union troops.

A Confederate officer and a private from Florida.

A Florida Southern Railroad train at a station in Punta Gorda, Florida.

Before the 1880s, Florida's economy was built on agriculture. But in 1881, the mining of phosphate began. Phosphate is used in cattle feed and fertilizer. The lumber industry also grew. In the 1880s, the railroads came to Florida, so businesses and population increased after that. It was then that tourism began.

In the 1920s, thousands of people rushed to move to Florida. But the Great Depression, beginning in 1929, made life difficult. Many people lost their jobs, and few people had extra money.

As America's involvement in World War II began in 1941, the United States military built bases in Florida. This helped Florida's economy. The state's population has continued to grow since World War II. This includes Easterners, Southerners, Cubans, Latin Americans, and people retiring from the North. It makes Florida a place of many different cultures.

Soldiers train for hand-to-hand combat at Camp Blanding, Florida, in 1941.

Did You Know?

The city of St. Augustine, Florida, is the oldest non-Native American city in the United States. It has been occupied since 1565.

The Spanish explorer Juan Ponce de León landed there in 1513. He declared

St. Augustine, Florida, has many old buildings and cemeteries.

that Spain owned all of Florida, even though there were thousands of Native Americans living there.

The Spanish built a fort called Castillo de San Marcos. Construction began in 1672 and was finished in 1695. It is still standing today. It is a national monument.

St. Augustine has seen its share of battles. The city was destroyed by Sir Francis Drake in 1586, burned in 1702, and attacked in 1740. The British used the city during the Revolutionary War. It was used as a prison in the wars against the Seminole Indians. Union troops occupied it during the Civil War.

Today, St. Augustine has a population of 12,284. The city's Castillo de San Marcos Fort, as well as other Spanish buildings and museums, are popular places for tourists to visit.

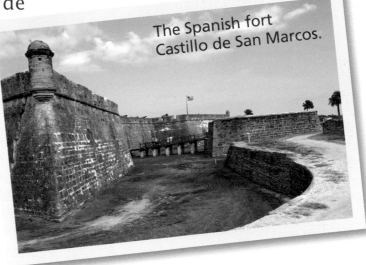

The Spanish fort Castillo de San Marcos.

People

Osceola (1804?-1838) was a Seminole war chief. His name means *black drink singer,* named after a black liquid made with holly leaves. In 1835, the United States government tried to force Seminoles off their land and move them to Oklahoma. Osceola led the battles against the U.S. Army. At first, the Native Americans were successful. Then, in 1837, the U.S. military invited Osceola to a peace conference. When the war chief arrived, he was seized and imprisoned. He died of malaria a few months later. A county in Florida and several cities around the United States were named in his honor.

Jacqueline Cochran (1906?-1980) was an American pilot. She held more speed records, distance records, and high altitude records than anyone else before her. She lived in Pensacola, Florida, and began flying in 1932. She won several airplane races in the 1930s. During World War II, she trained more than 1,000 female pilots for non-combat flights. She was awarded the Distinguished Service Medal. After World War II, she became the first woman to break the sound barrier, and continued to set other records. After her retirement, she served as a consultant to NASA.

Sidney Poitier (1927-) is an actor and director. He was born in Miami and spent much of his childhood in Florida. He began to act in Hollywood movies before there were many African American actors in film. In 1958, he was the first African American man to be nominated for an Academy Award, for *The Defiant Ones*. He was also the first African American man to win an Academy Award for his 1963 movie *Lilies of the Field*.

Gloria Estefan (1957-) is a singer and songwriter. She was born in Cuba, but her family fled to Miami when Gloria was a baby. Estefan began her singing career in the 1980s. She became very successful with many hit singles and best-selling albums. However, in 1990, she suffered a broken back in a serious traffic accident. After surgeries and a year of physical therapy, she returned to the stage. She continues to perform and work for charities. She has won dozens of awards for her music and good deeds.

Cities

Jacksonville is located in the northeastern part of Florida. It is the state's largest city, with a population of 805,605. Timucua Indians settled the area more than 6,000 years ago. Europeans founded the city in 1791, naming it Cowford. It was later renamed Jacksonville, after President Andrew Jackson. Today, it is an important port for ships on the Atlantic Ocean. Many colleges are located in Jacksonville, including the University of North Florida. The Jacksonville area is home to many major businesses, as well as several military bases. The military is the city's largest employer.

Tallahassee is the capital of Florida, with a population of 168,979. The city is both an agricultural center, as well as a home to many engineering and legal firms. Tallahassee is also the home of Florida State University and Florida A&M University.

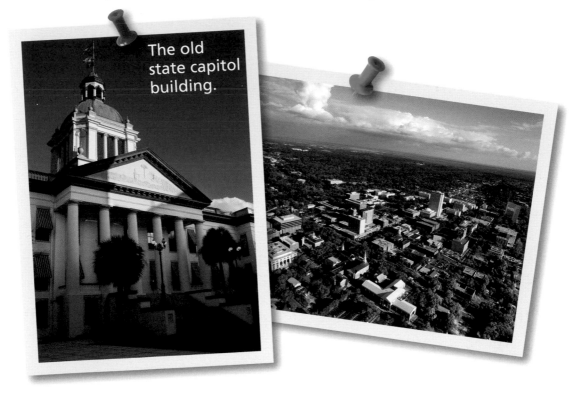

The old state capitol building.

The city of **Tampa** sits by an inlet of water called Tampa Bay. Tampa, St. Petersburg, Clearwater, and other cities surround the bay. This is called the Tampa Bay Area, or just the Bay Area. The Calusa and Timucua Indians originally settled the land. Today, the Tampa Bay Area has almost three million people. This makes it Florida's largest metro area on the Gulf Coast. The city of Tampa has 336,823 people.

Miami is at the southern tip of Florida, just east of the Everglades. The city has a population of 409,719. When counting all the  surrounding cities and towns, the metro population jumps to about four million. The Tequesta Indians first inhabited the area. They called it *mayaimi*, which may mean "big water." This may be a reference to nearby Lake Okeechobee. The United States military built a fort there in 1836, and the town grew around it. Today, the city is an important place for banking, tourism, research and international shipping. The University of Miami and other colleges are located in Miami.

Transportation

Interstate 10 goes east and west across the northern part of the state. Interstate 4 goes east and west at the central

The Overseas Highway.

part of the state. Interstates 75 and 95 go north and south through the state. Interstate 75 cuts to the east and west at Naples to Fort Lauderdale. The Overseas Highway is a 128-mile (206-km) road that goes out across the ocean, connecting the islands of the Florida Keys and ending at Key West. It is also part of U.S. Route 1.

Florida has 14 deepwater ports, which are harbors for big, heavy ships. There are many other ports in the state for smaller boats.

One of the busiest airports in the nation is Miami International Airport. From there, people travel to islands in the Caribbean, to Central and South America, and hundreds of other places. Other big airports include Orlando International, Tampa International, Palm Beach International, and Fort Lauderdale-Hollywood International.

People in the Everglades use an unusual type of transportation called an airboat. It has a flat bottom and a giant propeller in the back. Boaters use it to get across shallow swamps and marshy grasses.

An airboat crosses the Florida Everglades.

Natural Resources

Florida has many natural resources. It has ocean resources, farmland resources, and, of course, the warm weather is one of the state's most important resources.

Sunny Florida.

There are more than 40,000 farms in Florida, mostly in the north and central parts of the state. Farms cover about 10 million acres (4 million hectares).

Oranges are Florida's number one crop. The climate is especially good for citrus fruits. Citrus trees need lots of sunshine and no freezing temperatures. Florida farmers also grow sugarcane, grapefruit, strawberries, tangerines, and tomatoes. Farmers raise cattle and chickens, as well.

Oranges are Florida's number one crop.

Commercial fishing continues in Florida, but it is not as common as it once was.

Several minerals are mined in Florida. The most important has been phosphate, used in fertilizer and food for cattle. Other minerals mined include sand, limestone, sulfur, and peat. Florida also produces petroleum and natural gas.

Phosphate is one of Florida's most important natural resources.

Industry

In the late 1800s, citrus farming, phosphate mining, and lumber milling made up the economy. Tourism had just begun. Today, tourism is the biggest part of Florida's economy.

The rise in tourism has also helped other businesses to grow. Industries such as restaurants, transportation, construction, and retail sales have grown with tourism.

Agriculture continues to be a big part of Florida's economy. Manufacturing plays a smaller part in the state's economy. Products manufactured in the state are computers, electronic parts, transportation equipment, wood, and paper products. Citrus products, such as orange juice, are also manufactured in Florida.

Florida's large military bases bring in many jobs.
The John F. Kennedy Space Center at Cape Canaveral
is where spaceships carry astronauts into orbit. NASA
is a big
employer
of Florida
residents.

The John F. Kennedy Space
Center at Cape Canaveral
employs many Florida
residents. It is also a
popular spot for people
to visit. Many tourists
come to watch spaceships
take off or land.

Sports

There are many professional sports teams in Florida. National Football League teams are the Miami Dolphins, the Jacksonville Jaguars, and the Tampa Bay Buccaneers. These Florida teams have won many championships. The Dolphins and the Buccaneers have also won Super

Bowl titles. The Miami Heat and the Orlando Magic are National Basketball Association teams.

Professional baseball teams in Florida are the Marlins and the Tampa Bay Rays. Many sports teams from across the United States hold their spring practices in Florida because of the nice weather.

The FedEx Orange Bowl, a college football postseason game, is played every January in Miami.

The Daytona 500 is a famous automobile race held in Daytona Beach every February.

Boating, swimming, diving, and golf are always popular. People also enjoy deep-sea fishing and freshwater fishing.

The Daytona 500 is also known as "The Great American Race." It is 500 miles (805 km) or 200 laps around the track. It is one of the biggest NASCAR (National Association for Stock Car Auto Racing) races in the nation.

Entertainment

Thousands of people visit Florida's resorts and theme parks every day.

Walt Disney World Resort near Orlando is one of the biggest tourist stops in the United States. It has many rides and activities. SeaWorld in Orlando features many ocean animals. It is a place for education, research, and fun rides. At Busch Gardens in Tampa, people watch African animals. The John F. Kennedy Space Center is also a very popular stop for visitors.

At Universal Studios Florida, visitors can see how movies are made, and go on interesting rides. Disney's Hollywood Studios in Lake Buena Vista offers fun activities featuring Disney characters.

For those who like the outdoors, Florida has 3 national parks, 110 state parks, and many national monuments and seashores.

A family takes a picture at the JAWS ride at Universal Studios Florida.

There are many state festivals and theaters. There are pirate festivals, historical museums, and art houses. There is no limit of things to do in Florida. The state is perhaps the biggest vacation stop in the country.

Timeline

10,000 BC—Native Americans live in the area that will become Florida.

1513—Ponce de Leon's first visit.

1521—Ponce de Leon's second visit. Native Americans stop him from settling the area.

1565—The city of St. Augustine is founded.

1845—Florida becomes the 27th state in the Union.

1861—Florida leaves the Union and joins the Confederacy. The Civil War begins.

1920s—People rush to claim land in Florida.

1962—NASA builds the Launch Operations Center on Florida's east coast. It is later renamed the Kennedy Space Center.

1971—Walt Disney World Resort opens with the Magic Kingdom theme park.

1973—The Miami Dolphins win their first Super Bowl.

1981—*Columbia* is the first space shuttle launched from Kennedy Space Center.

2003—Tampa Bay Buccaneers win the Super Bowl. Florida Marlins win the World Series.

Glossary

Citrus—Referring to fruits such as oranges, lemons, limes, and grapefruits.

Civil War—The war fought between the Northern and Southern states from 1861-1865. The Southern states were for slavery. They wanted to start their own country. Northern states fought against slavery and a division of the country.

Confederacy—A group of 11 Southern states that broke away from the United States during the Civil War, which lasted from 1861 until 1865.

Malaria—A serious, sometimes fatal, tropical disease. People get malaria when an infected mosquito bites them.

NASA (National Aeronautics and Space Administration)—A U.S. government agency started in 1958. NASA's goals include space exploration, as well as increasing people's understanding of Earth, our solar system, and the universe. One major NASA facility is the John F. Kennedy Space Center in Florida.

Panhandle—A narrow strip of land that juts out from the rest of the state. Florida's panhandle is made up of the state's 16 westernmost counties.

Peninsula—Land with water on three sides.

Phosphate—A mineral used in fertilizer and food for cattle.

Revolutionary War—The war fought between the American colonies and Great Britain from 1775-1783. It is also known as the War of Independence or the American Revolution.

Seminole—Native Americans made up of various Creek Indian tribes who moved into Florida during the 1700s and 1800s.

Swamp—An area that is always wet, usually overgrown with grasses, bushes, and trees.

World War II—A conflict across the world, lasting from 1939-1945. The United States entered the war in December 1941.

Index